THE Silly JOKE BOOK

by Victoria Hartman

Illustrated by Don Orehek

SCHOLASTIC INC.
New York Toronto London Auckland Sydney

For Laura and Vittorio

ISBN 0-590-33846-3

12 11 10 9 8 7 6 5 4 3 2 1   7 8 9/8 0 1 2/9

Printed in the U.S.A.   01

First Scholastic printing, March 1987

THE Silly JOKE BOOK

ANIMAL WARM-UPS

How do robins get in shape?

They do worm-ups.

Where do cows hang their paintings?

In moo-seums.

How can you tell if a tyrannosaurus
is asleep?

By the dino-snores.

What happens when a colt whinnies
too much?

It becomes hoarse.

What do you call the sale of a lion?

A roar deal.

What do birds eat for breakfast?

Shredded tweet.

What is an owl's favorite TV program?

Little Whoos on the Prairie.

What do snake charmers wear around their necks?

Boa-ties.

What do you call a cocoon who
hates parties?

A party pupa.

What kind of bugs bother violinists?

Fiddles-ticks.

What kind of TV programs do wild animals like?

Game shows.

What kind of bears like to go out in the rain?

Drizzly bears.

What do you call the winner of a
beauty contest for sheep?

Miss Ewe-niverse.

What kind of spiders live in Iran?

Tehran-tulas.

What kind of math do owls like?

Owl-gebra.

What do snakes learn in school?

Reading, writing, and arithmetic.

Why did the itchy dog think he was a sheep?

He had fleece.

Why do some kangaroos grow up to be crooks?

They start off with a peek-pocket.

What crook lives in the ocean?

The mobster lobster.

Why was the dolphin so sad?

It had no porpoise in life.

Why did the buffalo think that 1976 was their year?

It was the bison-tennial.

What kind of fish likes to borrow books?

A library cod.

How does a fish pay his bills?

With a credit cod.

JOKES YOU'LL EAT UP

What's the best cheese to eat when you are up a tree?

Limb-burger cheese.

What kind of cheese does a dog like on his pizza?

Mutts-arella.

What does a grump put on his toast?

Gripe jelly.

What do you call a lost hot dog?

The missing link.

What do healthy ghosts eat
for breakfast?

Hex Chex.

What is an Australian ghost's favorite dessert?

Boo-meringue pie.

What's a duck's favorite dish?

Quackeroni and cheese.

When does a cucumber laugh?

When it's a tickled pickle.

What do you call frightened flapjacks?

Griddle quakes.

Where do cows go for lunch?

The calf-eteria.

27

What kind of pie sticks to your ribs?

Glue-berry pie.

What do you call the battle between
Coca-Cola and Pepsi-Cola?

A fizz fight.

What kind of cookies do gnus eat?

Fig gnutons.

What state has the smallest containers
of soft drinks?

Mini-soda.

What do you call hamburger fights?

Meat brawls.

What can you eat on a starvation diet?

Fast food.

What is an elf's favorite food?

Lepre-corn.

What do you call people who
sell cornmeal?

Pone brokers.

What do you call thirteen sleeping
pastry chefs?

Bakers dozin'.

What's a monster's favorite snack?

Dread and butter.

What is the favorite cookie of Baltimore baseball fans?

Baltimore Oreos.

GHOULY GIGGLES

How does a witch break the sound barrier?

With a sonic broom.

Which kind of witch turns out
the lights?

A lights witch.

What do you call a house with
two patios?

An extra-terrace-trial.

Why can you rely on Count Dracula in a crisis?

Because he's ghoul, calm, and collected.

What monster never knocks?

The Knock-less Monster.

How does an actor get a part in a horror movie?

He passes a scream test.

Why do ghosts like health food?

Because it's super-natural.

What did one devil say to the other?

Any fiend of yours is a fiend of mine.

Where do French ghosts sleep?

In the boo-doir.

Where do fashionable ghosts go
shopping?

In a boo-tique.

Where do monsters get their education?

At the little red ghoul house.

What did the coach say to the losing
ghost team?

Where's that ol' team spirit?

44

Why did Dracula go to the circus?

He liked to see the acro-bats.

What do you call very small detectives?

Sherlock Gnomes.

What is the favorite ride of the
phantom of the amusement park?

The roller-ghoster.

Where do French monsters like to go for supper?

A beastro.

Where do witches keep their pet fish?

In an eeek-quarium.

How does a witch tell time?

With a witch watch.

In what desert do monsters live?

In the Sa-horror Desert.

How do monsters move their furniture?

With U-Howl trucks.

RIDICULOUS TALES

How did Sir Lancelot see in the dark?

He used a knight light.

Where do lizards write their stories?

In loose-leaf newtbooks.

What did the Three Little Pigs sing
when they were in Arabia?

Who's Afraid of the Baghdad Wolf?

What is a gardener's first book?

A beginning weeder.

Why did Sir Lancelot keep swatting himself?

Because of the Gnats of the Round Table.

Why was Aladdin interested in his family tree?

He was a genie-ologist.

Why was the author so happy to live in a basement?

It was a best-cellar.

What do you call the author of a
Western story?

A horseback writer.

Why didn't the rock climbers want to listen to the storyteller?

Because they had been warned about the ledge-end.

What kind of mysteries do owls read?

Whoo-dunnits.

What else besides the Seven Dwarfs whistles while it works?

A teapot.

What does Santa use for bandages?

Santa Gauze.

Why did Robin Hood let everyone cut down trees in his forest?

It was Share-wood Forest.

What does everyone wait for the week before Christmas?

The present moment.

What do you eat after you trim the tree?

Deco-rations.

What is Santa's favorite candy?

Jolly beans.

UTTER NONSENSE

What do you call someone who bites a police officer?

A *law a-biting citizen.*

What does a doctor use to listen to a sneaky crook's heart?

A *stealth-o-scope.*

What do you call a lineup at the haircutters?

A barber-queue.

What kind of sweaters do singers wear?

Croon-neck sweaters.

Where do farmers get their
prescriptions filled?

At the farmer-cy.

What kind of tree should you plant
outside a drugstore?

A chemist tree.

What do you call the person who trains
a prince?

An heir-conditioner.

Where does a crook fill his gas tank?

At the villain station.

What is the difference between a
lottery player and a cowpoke?

One draws lots and the other drawls lots.

Why do some people never go bald?

They have a re-seeding hairline.

On which cuff does a comedian write his jokes?

The one on his humor wrist.

What does the stock market have in common with a pogo stick?

They both have their ups and downs.

How does a code breaker make
a decision?

He has to decipher himself.

What did the architect say when she
was thanked for a job well done?

Don't mansion it.

What do you call twin boys?

A son-set.

What is the difference between a
person with a cold and a prizefighter?

*One blows his nose, the other knows
his blows.*

What do you call a prizefighter's boast?

A punching brag.

What do you call a party held in the basement?

A cellar-bration.

What do you call a sheet salesman?

An undercover agent.

Why do you have to be careful if a dentist offers you a drink?

It might be a molar-tov cocktail.

What's the difference between a smart aleck and a boy's question?

One is a wise guy. The other is a guy's why.

Why do some drivers have good safety records?

Because they are wreck-less.

What's the best cleanser to use in outer space?

Halley's Comet.

What is the difference between
a mixed-up deck of cards,
a dressmaker who is out of glitter,
and a baseball player?

*The cards are out of sequence;
the dressmaker is out of sequins;
the baseball player is out to seek wins.*

What kind of perfume do
teenagers like?

Adole-scents.

What is the worst game to bring to the desert?

Parch-eesi.

What can you wear to a masquerade party?

Disguise the limit.

What's the difference between ten years
and a bad tooth?

*Ten years is a decade and a rotten tooth
is decayed.*

Where is the best place to build
a railroad?

On choo-choo terrain.

What do you call a wig fitting?

A tress rehearsal.

COMPUTER COMICS

What is a duck's favorite video game?

Quack Man.

What do computer experts eat for
a snack?

Memory chips.

Why did the computer programmer
have trouble playing frisbee?

He had a floppy disc.

How do you make friends with
a computer?

Bit by bit.

How does a drowning Atari get
to shore?

With a comput-oar.

What do computers eat for lunch?

Floppy Joes and Micro Chips.

Why did the computer cross the road?

To get to the other sine.

What's a computer's favorite dessert?

Bananalog.

How did the computers afford
a vacation?

They all chipped in.

What do British computers eat
for lunch?

Fiche and chips.

Where do computers go on
Saturday night?

To a disc-o.

How do computers get stronger?

Pumping Ion.

LAST LAUGHS

What do you call a genuine rowboat?

Oar-thentic.

How do you divide the ocean?

With a sea-saw.

What kind of hats do sailors from Texas wear?

Ten galleon hats.

What kind of boat do all families own?

A kinship.

What do you call an old drip?

An ex-spurt.

What is a camper's favorite
late-night snack?

A bed-roll.

What do campers like to see?

A camp-sight.

What do campers eat on a hike?

March-mallows.

How do climbers hear?

With mountain-ears.

What kind of jacket do you wear
on a hike?

A trail blazer.